"A very scriptural foundation and eye-opening teaching from the Book of Genesis."

Dr. Ronald L. Diggs,
Pastor, High Point, NC

"A delightful way to teach the Genesis Story!"

Emily Petersen,
School Counselor, Reidsville, NC

"It teaches kids that God created us. We just didn't pop up. He spoke and everything came in place."

Hailey Wilson,
4th grade, Greensboro, NC
Hailey is nine years old

"Thank-You LORD for creating the earth, the animals and for making all the kind people."

Christian Smith,
2nd grade, Greensboro NC
Christian is seven years old

"This is a great book that can appeal to all ages who want to learn about the creation of the world. I will read this book to my grandchildren and other children."

Annie Spain,
Retired Bank Vice-President

It Was All Done in Six Days
Copyright © 2009 by Gayle Graves. All rights reserved.

This title is also available as a Tate Out Loud product. Visit www.tatepublishing.com for more information.

No part of this publication may be reproduced, stored in a retrieval system or transmitted in any way by any means, electronic, mechanical, photocopy, recording or otherwise without the prior permission of the author except as provided by USA copyright law.

Scripture taken from the Amplified Bible, Copyright © 1954, 1958, 1962, 1964, 1965, 1987 by The Lockman Foundation. Used by permission.

Scripture taken from the New King James Version®. Copyright © 1982 by Thomas Nelson, Inc. Used by permission. All rights reserved.

[Holy Bible, Contemporary English Version, copyright 1995, American Bible Society, Printed in the United States of America]

Book design copyright © 2009 by Tate Publishing, LLC. All rights reserved.

The opinions expressed by the author are not necessarily those of Tate Publishing, LLC.

Published by Tate Publishing & Enterprises, LLC
127 E. Trade Center Terrace | Mustang, Oklahoma 73064 USA
1.888.361.9473 | www.tatepublishing.com

Tate Publishing is committed to excellence in the publishing industry. The company reflects the philosophy established by the founders, based on Psalm 68:11,
"The Lord gave the word and great was the company of those who published it."

Book design copyright © 2009 by Tate Publishing, LLC. All rights reserved.
Cover and Interior design by Eddie Russell
Illustration by Benton Rudd

Published in the United States of America

ISBN: 978-1-61566-018-6
Juvenile Nonfiction: Poetry: Nursery Rhymes
09.09.22

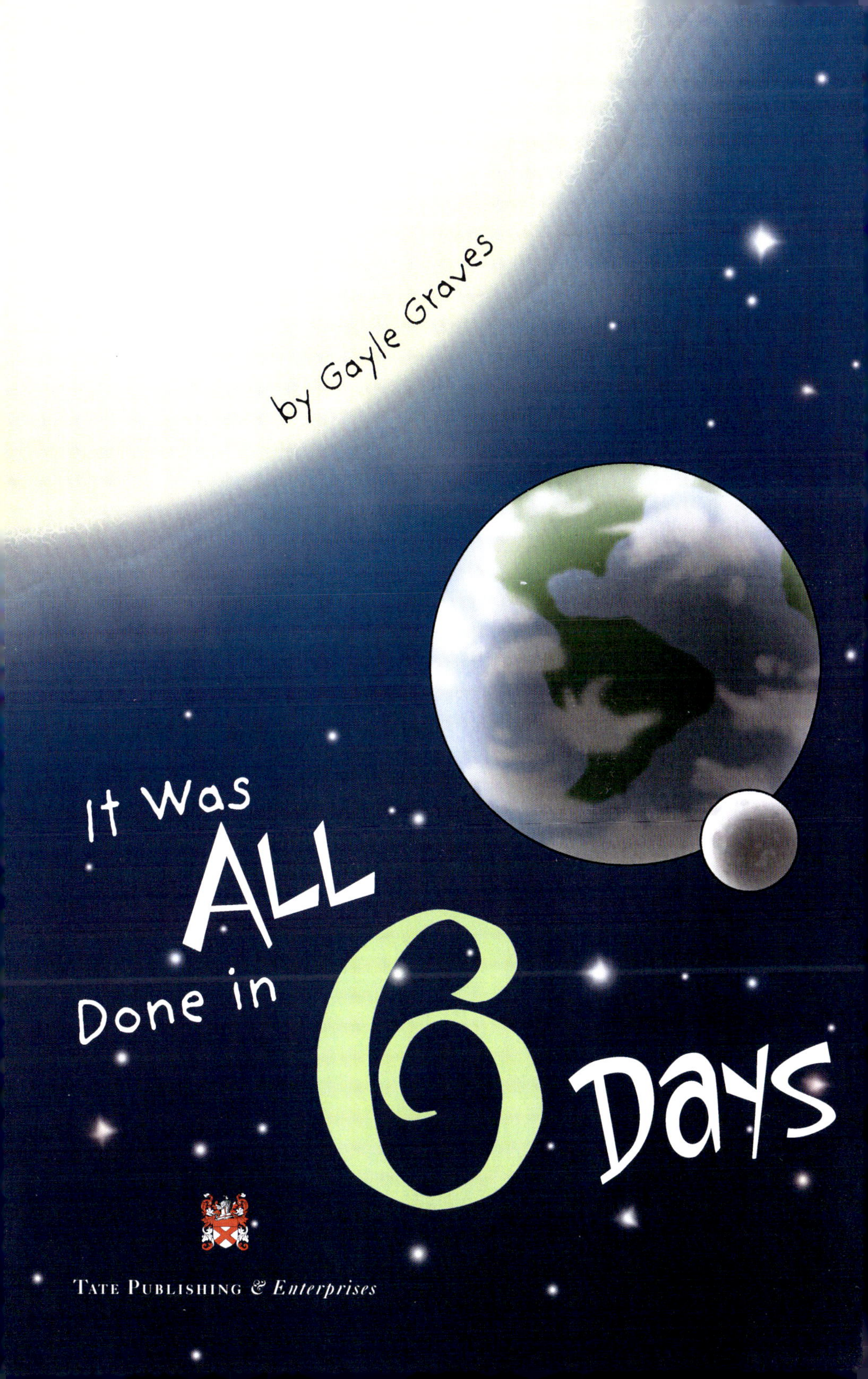

by Gayle Graves

It Was
ALL
Done in
6 Days

Tate Publishing & Enterprises

The earth was without form;
everything was all mixed up.
It was like everything was shaken
and poured out of a coffee cup.
The dirt and rocks were everywhere.
Everything was a mess! And where was the air?

The light and darkness were all mingled together;
the misplaced water did not make it any better.
God looked around and saw all of that mess.
He said,

"I know what to do and I'll do what is best."

God told the darkness to get away from the light.
He just spoke it; He didn't have to fight.
The light appeared and God said,

"OH! THIS IS GOOD."

And the darkness went where it knew it should.

God called the light "day"
and darkness He called "night."
The Spirit of God moved and did everything right.
God is All Powerful. He knows what to say,
so the evening and morning were the very first day.

GENESIS 1:1–5

Now the darkness and light are in the right place,
and God said,

"I'll take the sky with water and give it its space."

God began to speak with a lot of love.
He told the sky with water, "You dwell above."

And to the rest of the waters so you can flow,
you gather together and dwell below.
God is All Powerful. He knows what to say,
so the evening and morning were the
second day.

Genesis 1:6-8

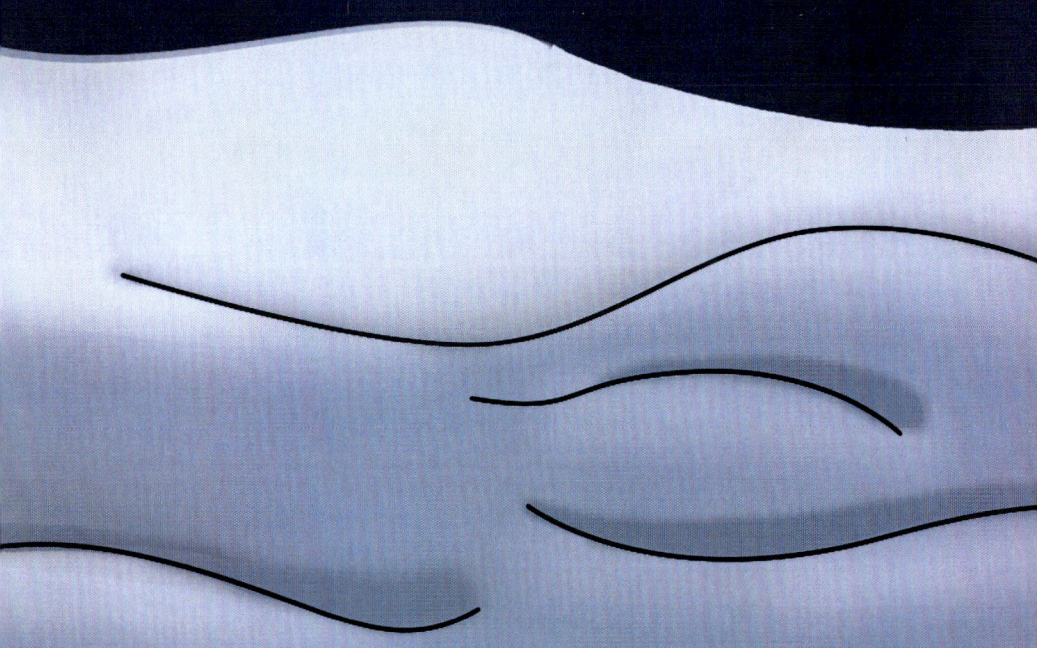

God told the waters that were below,
"I have a special place for you to go.
You are to go here, there, and over here,
then there will be space for dry land to appear."

So the gathering of the waters God called "seas,"
and the dry land He called "earth,"
all done with ease.
All things God spoke were done as they should,

And God was pleased and said,

"Oh! This is good."

God told the earth to produce herbs,
plants, and fruit trees,
including vegetations, probably broccoli and peas.
God is All Powerful. He knows what to say,
so the evening and morning were the third day.

Genesis 1:9–13

God looked around and saw that everything was right.
Then He boldly said, "Let there be lights."
These powerful lights divided the day from the night.
These lights were so awesome. Oh! What a sight!

The awesome lights were placed in the big, big, sky.
They went where God told them, not too low or high.
The sun, moon, and stars had such a powerful glow.
Their radiant beams gave light on the big earth below.

The sun is the big light that rules in the day.
The moon is the lesser light that rules the night's way.
God created countless stars
and knows all of them by name.
All of the stars are different; none of them are the same.

The lights are for signs, seasons, days, and years.
God was pleased with His work; He never fears.
God is All Powerful. He knows what to say,
so the evening and morning were the fourth day.

Genesis 1:14–19

Now, the mighty seas that were on the earth,
the Spirit of God was moving
and beginning to create birth.
God told the waters to abound
with a lot of creatures
like whales and fish
with different kinds of features.

Next, God told the birds to fill the earth and sky.
Then, He told the birds and sea creatures
to be fruitful and multiply.
God is All Powerful. He knows what to say,
so the evening and morning
were the fifth day.

Genesis 1:20-23

The waters below were filled
with an abundance of sea life.
The sea creatures played and there was no strife.
The dry land and sky had no other living things,
only birds that loved to fly and sing, sing, sing.

God said,
"Let there be
more living things—
cattle, beast, living creatures,
and some with wings."
The living things appeared in all kinds of places,
filling up the earth's lonely and empty spaces.

The abundance of living things did as they should.
God was pleased and said,
"Oh! This is good."
He told the living things, as He passed by,
to be fruitful so they could multiply.

There were different living things
throughout the land.

Then God said,
"It is time to make man."
God made man that looked like Him.
Male and female, God created them.

God showed them everything He had done.
And told them to rule over everything under the sun.
God was pleased with the earth, sea, and the sky.
Then He told man to be fruitful and multiply.

God showed man all the good foods to eat,
some on big trees and a lot at his feet.
There was food for the cattle, beast,
and other living things,
even food for the sea creatures
and the birds with wings.

God saw everything that he had made.
Indeed it was very good, even the nice cool shade.
It was all done in six days.
Everything was perfect there were no delays.

All of God's creation is in His hands.
He spoke it all into existence, even man.
God is All Powerful. He knows what to say,
so the evening and the morning were the sixth day.

Genesis 1:24-31

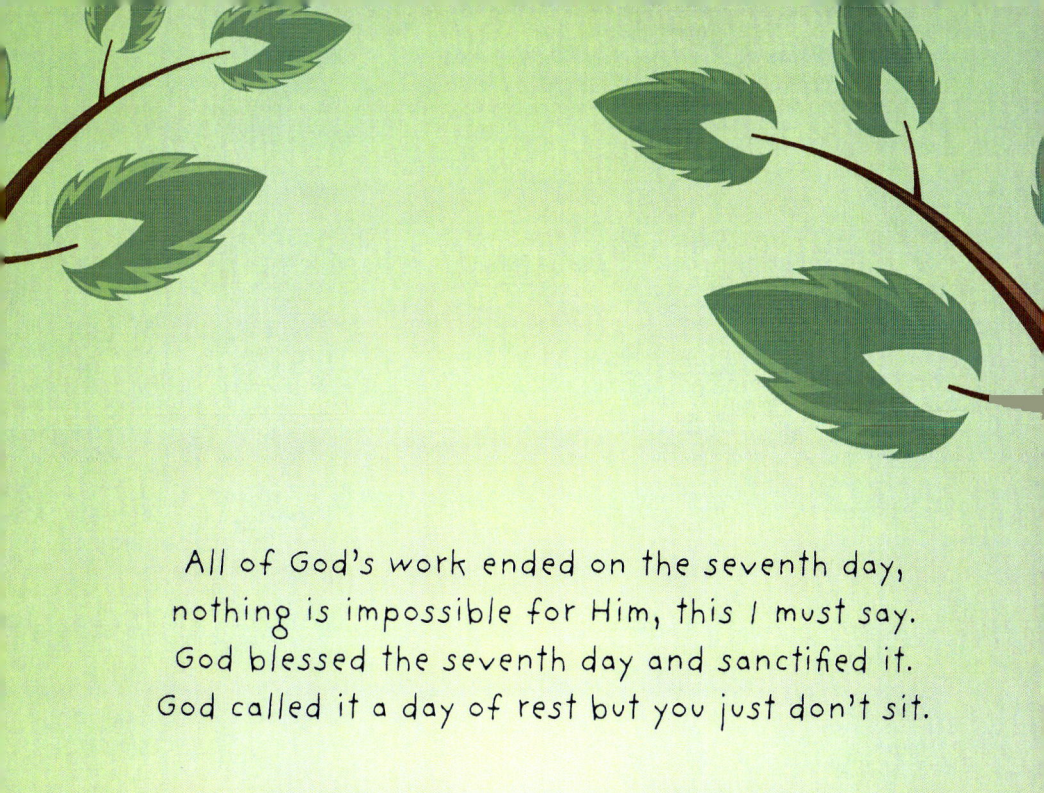

All of God's work ended on the seventh day,
nothing is impossible for Him, this I must say.
God blessed the seventh day and sanctified it.
God called it a day of rest but you just don't sit.

It is a day we rest from our busy week.
And remember it is God whom we must seek.
A time to be still and give thanks
for what He's done.
God, the Creator of the universe,
He is the only one.

God is not selfish. He does not ask much.
He knows what He is doing
and has the perfect touch.
He gave us six days to work and for some to play.
He only asks for Himself just one lonely day.

Now don't forget when we work five or six days,
to keep God in our hearts, there are no other ways.
Remember, God is love and let His love abide in us.
We are to love everyday, and don't put up a fuss.

Genesis 2:2-4

The Beginning

listen|imagine|view|experience

AUDIO BOOK DOWNLOAD INCLUDED WITH THIS BOOK!

In your hands you hold a complete digital entertainment package. Besides purchasing the paper version of this book, this book includes a free download of the audio version of this book. Simply use the code listed below when visiting our website. Once downloaded to your computer, you can listen to the book through your computer's speakers, burn it to an audio CD or save the file to your portable music device (such as Apple's popular iPod) and listen on the go!

How to get your free audio book digital download:

1. Visit www.tatepublishing.com and click on the e|LIVE logo on the home page.
2. Enter the following coupon code:
   92d0-3185-5afc-037f-b98b-f210-e00f-f57f
3. Download the audio book from your e|LIVE digital locker and begin enjoying your new digital entertainment package today!